Social Skills Learning

Social Skills Learning

Naomi Samuel

Session plans and practical activities

www.loggerheadpublishing.co.uk

First published in 2016 by
Loggerhead Publishing Ltd, PO Box 928, Northampton NN7 9AP, United Kingdom
Tel: 01604 870828 International Tel: +44 1604 870828
Fax: 01604 870986 International Fax: +44 1604 870986

www.loggerheadpublishing.co.uk

© Sensory Learning & Play C.I.C. 2016

All rights reserved. The whole of this work including all text and illustrations is protected by copyright. No part of it may be copied, altered, adapted or otherwise exploited in any way without express prior permission, unless in accordance with the provisions of the Copyright, Designs and Patents Act 1988 or in order to photocopy or make duplicating masters of those pages so indicated, without alteration and including all copyright notices, for the express purpose of instruction. No parts of this work may otherwise be loaded, stored, manipulated, reproduced or transmitted in any form or by any means, electronic or mechanical, including photocopying and recording, or by any information storage and retrieval system, without prior written permission from the publisher, on behalf of the copyright owner.

Naomi Samuel has asserted her right to be identified as the author of this work.

Designed by Moo Creative (Luton)
Printed in the United Kingdom

British Library Cataloguing in Publication Data. A catalogue record for this book is available from the British Library

ISBN 978-1-909380-91-2

Contents

About the Author vi
Introduction 1

Activities

About Me 2
Rules 5
Feelings 7
Mixed Feelings 10
Just for Fun! 1 12
Boasting 13
We Are All Different 17
Empathy 22
Feeling Good 27
Just for Fun! 2 30
Honesty 31
Emotions 34
Saying 'Thank You' 39
Just for Fun! 3 42
Respecting Differences 43
Focus on Feelings 45
In Someone Else's Shoes 49
Paying Compliments 52
Just for Fun! 4 55
How do You Want to be Treated by Others? 56
Listening 58
Healthy Eating 61
Personal Hygiene 64
Just for Fun! 5 68
Growing Pains 69
Appropriate Language 72
What I Have Learned 75
Just for Fun! 6 77
Appendices 79
Workbook Cover 80
Pupil Tracking Sheet 81
Suggested Resources 82

About the Author

Naomi Samuel is a qualified social worker and teacher with over 11 years of experience in the social care and education sector. She specialises in working with children and young people with behavioural needs, learning needs and disabilities. Naomi is the co-founder of Look Inside Sensory Learning & Play which is a sensory play centre for children with additional needs and disabilities.

Introduction

Social Skills Learning contains basic session plans around one-hour long and worksheets on social skills which can be tailored to meet the needs of individual groups of children.

The book is a tool to teach children, particularly those with behavioural and learning needs, social skills for life as the lack of these skills can be a barrier to learning. The activities place high importance on teaching behaviour for learning and bridging the gap where social learning may not have taken place or needs demonstrating using a specialist approach. The book can be followed through from the beginning to the end or can be used as one-off sessions to meet the needs of the group/individual. All sessions have a plan which can be adapted to one-to-one or group sessions. It is a foundation from which you can be as creative as you would like with the topics and suggestions.

The front page of the workbook in the appendices can be used as a front sheet to make up a pupil's file. The appendices also include a Pupil Tracking Sheet to use for assessment purposes.

Note:
The activities are ideal for a group containing six to eight pupils but will work with other group sizes — you will be able to judge depending on how well you know your group, how long it has been established and so on.

About Me

Session aim

To describe personal identity

Objectives

1. To identify basic attributes for each pupil's personality
2. To explain likes and dislikes

Resources

- Masks (see page 3)
- Paint
- Paintbrushes

Session Plan

0 – 10 minutes	Ask the pupils to say one positive thing about their day and give them the opportunity to explain why if they would like to.
11 – 30 minutes	Give each pupil a mask and let them paint and design it however they want to, to show things which are significant to them.
31 – 50 minutes	Facilitate discussion about personal identity while the pupils paint their masks.
51 – 60 minutes	Pupils complete the About Me worksheet on their likes and dislikes with support if necessary.

Masks

Social Skills Learning

About Me

My age: ....

My likes:

My dislikes:

What I worry about at school:

Name: ....   Date: ....

Social Skills Learning

Rules

Session aim
To identify basic social rules

Objectives
1. To discuss what rules are used within school and the community
2. To think about why rules are important
3. To identify six rules for the group sessions

Resources
- Any board game
- Emotion cards showing faces (see Suggested Resources page 82 or you could make your own)
- Picture cards of people following rules and of people breaking the rules (see Suggested Resources page 82 or you could find your own, perhaps involving the pupils in a separate session prior to this activity)

Session Plan

0 – 25 minutes	Ask the pupils how their day has been and to identify one positive thing that has happened to them today. Play a board game with the group; make it clear what the rules are to ensure that there is always a link back to the topic of rules.
26 – 35 minutes	Facilitate a group discussion about what rules are, why they are needed and what effects they have in school. Questions should include: 1. Do you know what the word 'rules' means? (overview of the definition of the word rules) 2. Why do we need rules? 3. Do you follow the school rules? 4. How do rules make you feel? (use the faces cards) 5. What were the rules of the game? Discuss unwritten rules (social norms) - use the picture cards
36 – 50 minutes	Identify six rules for the group sessions.
51 – 60 minutes	Pupils complete the Rules worksheet.

Worksheet

Social Skills Learning

Rules

1.
2.
3.
4.
5.
6.

DON'TS

DO'S

Name: .... Date: ....

Activity

Social Skills Learning

Feelings

Session aim
To demonstrate feelings in practice

Objectives
1. To discuss types of feelings
2. To identify triggers for pupils' feelings
3. To think about strategies that can be used to help control emotions

Resources
- Emotion picture cards (faces) – see Suggested Resources page 82
- Emotion word cards to match the faces or visit www.mes-english.com/flashcards/feelings.php and use the handout
- Whiteboard
- Coloured paper
- Scissors
- Glue

Session Plan

0 – 25 minutes	Ask the pupils how their day has been and if anyone would like to share one good thing about it. Facilitate a group discussion about what feelings the pupils are aware of; use the emotion picture cards and link each word to the correct emotion face. Charades – show more picture cards with different emotions and ask a pupil to act out each emotion while the rest of the group identifies the emotion the picture portrays. Use a point/tally chart on the whiteboard. Extension – ask pupils to think of an emotion independently and to act it out.
26 – 40 minutes	Using the emotion picture cards, explain to the pupils they have to think about each question and answer by showing a card. There is no verbal communication from the pupils at this point. Questions could include: 1. How do you feel when you smile? 2. How do you feel when you cry? 3. How do you feel right now? 4. How would you feel if someone called you a horrible name? 5. How would you feel if you were told you are going to get a nice surprise or present? 6. How would you feel if you got a positive phone call home? 7. How would you feel if your teacher gave you a prize for good behaviour?

Social Skills Learning

41 – 60 minutes	Create a collage using coloured paper, scissors and glue to show the types of feelings each pupil experiences; each colour should represent a different emotion/feeling.
61 – 70 minutes	Pupils complete the Feelings worksheet with support from staff.

Social Skills Learning

Feelings

List four feelings you know:

1. ....

2. ....

3. ....

4. ....

I feel good when …

I feel frustrated when …

Strategies …

✓ ....

✓ ....

✓ ....

Name: .... Date: ....

Social Skills Learning

Mixed Feelings

Session aim
To explore mixed feelings

Objectives
1. To discuss what mixed feelings are
2. To identify situations where pupils have had mixed feelings

Resources
- Mixing bowl
- Feelings cards (https://childrenscenter.sa.ucsb.edu/CMSMedia/Documents/ParentSupport/FeelingWords.pdf)
- Mixing spoon
- Cake recipe
- Laptops
- Coloured paper
- Plain paper
- Pens, scissors and glue

Session Plan

0 – 10 minutes	Ask the pupils how their day has been and to share one positive thing about it.
11 – 40 minutes	Define mixed feelings (feeling more than two feelings in the same situation) e.g. first day at school - nervous, excited, worried. Use the mixing bowl and add feelings cards to it and stir with the spoon as pupils give their examples of when they have felt mixed feelings.
41 – 55 minutes	Give the pupils an example of a recipe about how to bake a cake and ask them to create a mixed-feelings recipe using pictures, words, laptops, pen and paper, scissors and glue.
56 – 60 minutes	Pupils complete the Mixed Feelings worksheet.

Mixed Feelings

What situation have you been in that has given you mixed feelings?

List the mixed feelings you experienced:

HAPPY BORED ANGRY

Name: .... Date: ....

Just for Fun! 1

Let's make music ...

What you need:

✓ Empty bottle

✓ Beads

✓ Rice

✓ Masking tape

✓ Scissors

✓ Newspaper

1. Cover the table with newspaper
2. Fill the empty bottle with beads and rice
3. Tape the lid on securely
4. Show us your music skills

✓ Use your shaker when you need to relax: maybe talk about times when it would come in handy ...

Boasting

Session aim
To demonstrate boasting

Objectives
1. To identify examples of boasting
2. To explain why people might boast
3. To discuss how boasting might make others feel

Resources
- Play dough
- Stop watch – real or online http://www.online-stopwatch.com/
- Word search (see page 15)
- Feelings cards (see Suggested Resources page 82)
- Red and green cards

Session Plan

0 – 20 minutes	Games time - explain to the pupils that they will have a set amount of time to complete each of the following games and the one with the most points at the end wins. If working one-to-one staff should join in with the games and boast (ask the pupils after how they felt about you boasting). Game 1 – Make an animal out of play dough and staff will judge the best one. (Use a stopwatch) Game 2 – Wordsearch - find as many words as you can in the wordsearch supplied on page 15. (Use a stopwatch) Game 3 – Staring contest - the first to blink loses!
21 – 35 minutes	Facilitate a group discussion using the feelings cards as necessary. Questions could include: 1. Have you ever boasted before? 2. Has anyone ever boasted to you? 3. How did that make you feel? 4. How do you think others feel when you boast to them? 5. When playing the games did anyone boast without realising? 6. Can we do this sometimes? 7. What should we do if we feel someone is boasting?

36 – 45 minutes	Give the pupils a green and red card each; explain that they need to show the red card if the statement you read is boasting and the green card if the statement read out is not boasting. Statements: 1. I am the best football player ever! 2. Check out my new bike! 3. I'm soo happy I have got a really good mark in my exam! 4. I got a new phone at Christmas. Have you still got that dead one from last year?!!! 5. Yes, I got full marks on my target card!
46 – 60 minutes	Pupils complete the Boasting worksheet with support from staff.

Social Skills Learning

Boasting Wordsearch

Y	I	L	S	W	H	D	O	N	L	Z	K
H	M	M	C	W	T	E	E	D	C	R	U
F	F	O	W	O	H	S	X	E	H	P	N
R	X	V	L	P	P	S	A	T	E	I	H
U	R	V	I	G	X	A	G	A	N	O	A
D	E	Z	D	A	V	R	G	R	H	R	P
E	T	K	K	A	U	R	E	T	Q	G	P
M	T	B	T	P	S	A	R	S	M	F	Y
X	E	T	S	X	Q	B	A	U	F	Z	K
Z	B	E	N	W	M	M	T	R	U	Z	M
W	T	U	U	C	A	E	E	F	A	H	H
A	N	N	O	Y	E	D	S	Q	I	R	R

ANNOYED
BETTER
EMBARRASSED
EXAGGERATE
FRUSTRATED
RUDE
SAD
SHOWOFF
UNHAPPY
UPSET

Name: .... Date: ....

Social Skills Learning

Boasting

Why do people boast?

....
....
....

Would boasting give you a comfortable feeling?

....
....
....

How does hearing someone boast make other people feel?

....
....
....

How might they behave?

....
....
....

What can we do if someone boasts a lot?

....
....
....

Name: .... Date: ....

Activity

Social Skills Learning

We Are All Different

Session aim
To show positive ways of dealing with differences

Objectives
1. To identify differences between pupils and others
2. To research beliefs of different cultures
3. To explain different strategies to use to ensure others do not feel judged because of their appearance/beliefs
4. To define bullying
5. To discuss what to do if you (or someone else) are being bullied

Note: This is a longer activity that could be run over two sessions if that would better suit your group

Resources
- Magazines
- Scissors, coloured paper, glue, pens/pencils
- Difference chart (see page 19)
- Matching activity (see page 20)
- Laptops/tablets
- Whiteboards and marker pens
- 'Say no to bullying' game (from the SEAL game resources or any other suitable game about bullying)
- Types of bullying information sheet (download something appropriate for your group from the Internet)

Session Plan

0 – 15 minutes	Ask the pupils how their day has been and to identify one positive thing about it. Explain that this session is sensitive and they may feel upset and can have a time out at any time. Remind them to be respectful about the words they use. Give the pupils the magazines and ask them to cut out 10 people and put them in pairs. Let them stick these onto coloured paper, then ask them to identify and write down at least one difference for each pair and one similarity. More able pupils should write down more differences.
16 – 30 minutes	Game time: give the pupils 10 minutes to ask as many people as possible the differences on the chart. Remind them to be polite.
31 – 50 minutes	Facilitate a group discussion. Explain that some differences people cannot see e.g. if someone cannot hear very well (hearing impairment). Ask the pupils to identify differences in the group that they cannot physically see.

51 – 60 minutes	Matching activity: ask the pupils to work in pairs to match each label to its definition. Stick them onto A4 paper and check the answers.
61 – 90 minutes	Research different cultures and religions using the laptop/tablet and make a PowerPoint presentation including: 1. Name of culture/religion 2. Three practices (e.g. praying) 3. Types of religious/cultural clothing worn 4. Different foods eaten 5. Different religious celebrations
91 – 110 minutes	Bullying - Play the 'Say no to bullying' game or your replacement game.
111 – 126 minutes	Ask the pupils to use whiteboards and write down as many types of bullying as they can think of (take a photo). Allow them to refer to the bullying information sheet if necessary.
127 – 141 minutes	Ask the pupils if they know how to use the school system to log a bullying incident in their school. Give them the opportunity to identify staff in school who they could tell about bullying. Refer back to prejudice and discrimination and how this is also a type of bullying.
142 – 156 minutes	Pupils complete the We Are All Different worksheet.

We Are All Different

No.	Name	M/F	Height	Hair Colour	Race
1					
2					
3					
4					
5					
6					
7					
8					
9					
10					

Social Skills Learning

Matching Activity

Equality	The state of being equal in status, rights and opportunities	**Ethnicity**	Belonging to a social group that has a common national or cultural tradition
Diversity	A range of differences	**Race**	A group of people sharing the same culture, history, language, skin colour etc; an ethnic group
Culture	The ideas, customs and social behaviour of a particular people or society	**Prejudice**	Dislike or hostility because of your opinion of their race, culture or religion
Tradition	A long-established custom or belief that has been passed on from one generation to another	**Discrimination**	Acting on your dislikes of somebody because of their differences

We Are All Different

What things make us different?

1. ....

2. ....

3. ....

What things make us special?

☺ ....

☺ ....

☺ ....

Bullying is

....

....

....

If I am being bullied I should

....

....

....

Name: .... Date: ....

Activity

Social Skills Learning

Empathy

Session aim
To explore examples of empathy

Objectives
1. To give three examples of showing empathy
2. To demonstrate empathy through role-play
3. To give one example of sympathy

Note: This is a longer activity that could be run over two sessions if that would better suit your group

Resources
- Morals game (SEAL resource) or any suitable substitute
- Empathy scenario (see page 23)
- Shoe template (see page 24), pens/pencils
- Empathy/Sympathy handout (see page 25)
- Expression cards (optional if you feel they would be useful for your group – see Suggested Resources or search for something suitable on the Internet)
- Magazines with empathy and sympathy images

Session Plan

0 – 15 minutes	Ask the pupils how their day has been and if they would like to share something positive. Start the session with the Morals game. During the game link it back to the topic by asking questions such as: • How do you think they feel and why? • How would you feel if you were them?
16 – 30 minutes	Read the empathy scenario to the pupils then give each pupil/pair a character. Ask them to write/draw emotions in the shoe as to how that person felt in this situation and why. Facilitate feedback.
31 – 45 minutes	Make an acrostic empathy poem.
46 – 64 minutes	Complete the Empathy/Sympathy handout individually to show the difference between empathy and sympathy. Facilitate feedback.
65 – 90 minutes	Pupils complete the Empathy worksheet with support if needed. (Use magazines for pictures.)

Empathy Scenario

Characters

1. Chantelle
2. Joseph
3. Solan
4. Victor
5. Teacher

That really hurt ...

- Chantelle got to her lesson late.
- Victor stuck his foot under the table so she tripped up.
- Chantelle swore at Victor.
- Victor got sent out of the lesson for tripping up Chantelle.
- The teacher asked Chantelle to sit next to Solan for now because the lesson had already started.
- Solan put her bag on the chair so that Chantelle could not sit next to her.
- Joseph threw a rubber at Solan.
- The teacher shouted at Joseph and gave him a detention for throwing things in the classroom.

Describe how each person feels in this scenario.

_____

Activity

Social Skills Learning

Shoe template

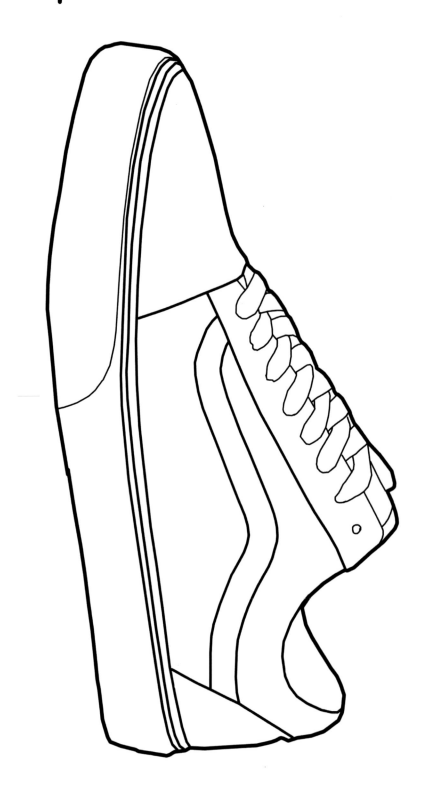

Empathy/Sympathy

Complete the definitions using the words below:

Empathy is the ……………… to……………………… and share the ……………… of another.

Sympathy is having feelings of ……………… and ………………………… for someone else's ………………………………………… .

pity	understand	ability
misfortune	feelings	sorrow

Social Skills Learning

Empathy

Empathy is

Sympathy is

Stick images of empathy below:

How do these pictures show empathy?

Name: Date:

Feeling Good

Session aim
Exploration of feeling good

Objectives
1. To identify what makes the pupils feel good
2. To recognise what makes other people feel good
3. To list three points of what feeling good means to the pupils

Resources
- A ball
- An open space
- Flashcards of positive activities (http://www.mes-english.com/flashcards/hobbies.php)

Session Plan

0 – 10 minutes	Ask the pupils if they would like to share one good thing about today.
11 – 30 minutes	Ball activity - What makes us feel good? and What makes others feel good? Go round the group and ask the first question then once each pupil has answered repeat with the other question. Bounce the ball to each other or roll the ball asking what we can do to make others feel good. The flashcards can be used to communicate what makes them or others feel good.
31 – 60 minutes	Pupils complete the Feeling Good worksheets.

Social Skills Learning

Feeling Good 1

What makes you feel good?

1. ....

2. ....

3. ....

Describe this feeling:

....
....

Do you ever feel like this at school?

....
....

How would you describe this feeling?

....
....

What can you do if you feel like this?

....
....

Name: .... Date: ....

Feeling Good 2

What would you do if you saw someone on their own at lunch or break time?

....

....

How could you make them feel good?

....

....

How do you feel when you are with friends?

....

....

I don't feel good when

....

....

Other people don't feel good when

....

....

Name: .... Date: ....

Just for Fun! 2

Let's squeeze our frustrations out ...

What you need:

✓ Resealable sandwich bags

✓ Beads, stars, shapes, rice

✓ Hair gel

✓ Food colouring

✓ Masking tape

✓ Scissors

✓ Newspaper

1. Cover the table with newspaper

2. Add the beads or other items to the bag

3. Add the hair gel

4. Add food colouring

5. Seal the bag and add tape so it is secure

✓ Can you think of a time when you may need to squeeze out your frustrations ...?

Honesty

Session aim
The importance of honesty

Objectives
1. To discuss pupils' understanding of what honesty means to them
2. To reflect on the value of honesty

Resources
- True and false cards (see page 32)
- Honesty statements e.g. "I ate breakfast this morning", "My hair is brown", "I like to go swimming"
- Shoe box
- Coloured paper
- Glue
- Scissors

Session Plan

0 – 10 minutes	Ask the pupils how their day has been and if they would like to share one good thing about it.
11 – 20 minutes	Ask them to recall what they had for a snack or lunch and praise them for being honest and telling the truth. Reiterate that honesty is speaking the truth.
21 – 30 minutes	Honesty game - each person has to say one thing which is true and one thing which is false and the rest of the group have to show if they think it is true or false using the true and false cards. Use honesty statements for support.
31 – 50 minutes	Honesty box - design an honesty box (it could be decorated with the coloured paper and glue) then use small slips of paper to write honesty statements on and put in the box. If appropriate for your group some statements could be read out.
51 – 60/65 minutes	Pupils complete the Honesty worksheet.

Activity

Social Skills Learning

True/False Cards

TRUE

FALSE

Social Skills Learning

Honesty

Have you ever been dishonest?

....
....

What happened because you were dishonest?

....
....
....

Why is it important to be honest?

....
....
....

Write your honesty goal below

....
....
....

Name: .... Date: ....

Social Skills Learning

Emotions

Session aim
Understanding emotions

Objectives
1. To discuss a variety of facial expressions
2. To be able to recognise three basic facial expressions
3. To attempt to demonstrate facial expressions

Resources
- Interactive games (http://www.kidvision.org/feelings/fun.html)
- Laptops

Session Plan

0 – 10 minutes	Ask the pupils how their day has been and if they would like to share one positive thing about it.
11 – 20 minutes	Working individually pupils use the facial expression interactive game to create and identify their own facial expressions.
21 – 30 minutes	In pairs they compare and contrast their creative facial expressions.
31 – 40 minutes	In groups pupils complete the feelings game online.
41 – 60 minutes	Pupils complete the four Emotions activity worksheets (you may wish to create your own if there are certain emotions that you would like your pupils to work on).

Emotions 1

How do these people feel?

1. ....

2. ....

3. ....

4. ....

Name: .... Date: ....

Emotions 2

How do these people feel?

5. ....

6. ....

7. ....

8. ....

Name: ....   Date: ....

Emotions 3

How do these people feel?

9. ....

10. ....

11. ....

12. ....

Name: .... Date: ....

Emotions 4

How do these people feel?

13. .... 14. ....

15. .... 16. ....

Name: .... Date: ....

Social Skills Learning

Saying 'Thank You'

Session aim
To identify the importance of saying 'Thank You'

Objectives
1. To identify three or more manners
2. To discuss why manners are important
3. To recall four times when pupils have said 'Thank You'

Resources
- Manners storybook (http://www.storyjumper.com/book/index/6901382/Mr-Manners-the-Bear)
- Scenario on manners (see page 40)
- Whiteboards

Session Plan

0 – 10 minutes	Ask the pupils how their day has been and to identify one positive thing about it.
11 – 20 minutes	Read the storybook on manners. Ask the pupils to say what they think manners are.
21 – 30 minutes	Read the scenario below where someone uses their manners and someone else does not. Ask the pupils to identify who is using their manners and who is not.
31 – 40 minutes	Make up some 'What if?' scenarios and ask the pupils to explain what they would do in that situation.
41 – 50 minutes	Ask the pupils to recall times when someone has said 'Thank You' to them.
51 – 60 minutes	Pupils complete the Saying 'Thank You' worksheet (use whiteboards to support spellings and understanding).

Scenario - Manners

John is rushing down the corridor. He is in a hurry because he is late for his lesson. He pushes past a teacher holding a pile of books and catches up with Mario, who is also late for the same lesson.

Mario holds the door open for the teacher who says, "Thank you." Mario replies, "You're welcome."

John shoves past and bursts through the door. He sits down and huffs. Mario walks in, walks up to the teacher quietly and says, "Sorry I am late." The teacher replies, "Thank you, Mario. Sit down please."

Social Skills Learning

Saying 'Thank You'

Think about the times you say 'Thank you'.

What happened?	Who did I say 'Thank you' to?

Name: .... Date: ....

Just for Fun! 3

Let it  out ...

What you need:

✓ Salt

✓ Paint

✓ Paintbrushes

✓ Newspaper

✓ PVA glue

✓ Glue stick

✓ Card

1. Cover the table with newspaper

2. Choose your card

3. Paste glue onto the card

4. Add salt in shapes or as lines

5. Paint the salt different colours

✓ Sometimes we hold on to things that make us feel sad. What needs to fizzle out in your life ...?

....

....

....

Respecting Differences

Session aim
To identify positive ways pupils can show they are respecting other people's differences

Objectives
1. To state one difference pupils have from others
2. To identify three ways to show pupils are respecting other people's opinions

Resources
- Football T-shirts/PE shirts

Session Plan

0 – 10 minutes	Ask the pupils how their day has been and to talk about one positive thing that has happened today.
11 – 20 minutes	Give the pupils the sports shirts and ask them to discuss and role-play: • Arguing about their favourite team • Respecting each other's opinions
21 – 40 minutes	Split the group in half and ask group A to think of a set of rules for giving your opinion frankly and group B to think of a set of rules which shows you are respecting other people's opinions.
41 – 60 minutes	Pupils complete the Respecting Differences worksheet.

Social Skills Learning

Respecting Differences

State one difference you have from others:

1 ....

Write a set of rules for:

A - Giving your opinion

1. ....

2. ....

3. ....

Write a set of rules for:

B - Respecting other people's opinions

1. ....

2. ....

3. ....

I can respect others by ....

....

Name: .... Date: ....

Activity

Focus on Feelings

Session aim
To put feelings into practice

Objectives
1. To identify how different occasions make the pupils feel
2. To identify how they are feeling at different times in the day

Resources
- List of occasions
- Emotions flashcards (see Suggested Resources page 82)
- My Feelings Timeline (see page 46)
- Feelings icons (see page 47)
- Glue

Session Plan

0 – 10 minutes	Ask the pupils how their day has been individually.
11 – 20 minutes	Give the pupils a list of occasions and ask them to explain how they make them feel and why (they should work in pairs). They can use the emotions flashcards to help them.
21 – 40 minutes	Give all the pupils the My Feelings Timeline sheet to complete - ask them to write down how they feel at different times in the day (you can extend/adapt the timeline to suit your group). Give them the feelings icons from page 47 to stick on as well.
41 – 60 minutes	Pupils complete the Focus on Feelings worksheet.

Social Skills Learning

My Feelings Timeline

Time	
7:30 am →	
8:30 am - School P1 →	
9:30am - P2 →	
10:30am - Break →	
11:00am - P3 →	
11:55am - P4 →	
12:55 - Lunch →	
1.40pm - P5 →	
2:10pm - P6 →	

Feelings Icons

Social Skills Learning

Focus on Feelings

How do these occasions make you feel?

Birthdays ....

First day at school ....

Seeing your friends ....

Being on your own ....

Draw a picture to show these feelings:

Happy   Sad

Worried   Confused

If someone said something horrible about me I would feel

....

....

Name: ....   Date: ....

Activity

Social Skills Learning

In Someone Else's Shoes

Session aim
Exploration of how other people feel

Objective
Identify three examples of when pupils would be empathetic

Resources
- Pictures of diverse people in different situations
- Emotions cards (see Suggested Resources page 82)
- Paint
- A3 paper
- Paintbrushes
- Scenarios

Session Plan

0 – 10 minutes	Ask the pupils how their day has been and to share one good thing about it.
11 – 25 minutes	Show the pupils the pictures and ask them how they would feel if it were them. Use the emotions cards as a point of reference.
26 – 40 minutes	Ask the pupils to paint emotion faces to demonstrate how other people may feel when a member of staff reads the scenario.
41 – 60 minutes	Pupils complete the In Someone Else's Shoes worksheet.

Scenarios – In Someone Else's Shoes

Jo is walking to school and Albert trips her up.

Alfie is eating his lunch and Patrick walks by and eats his chocolate bar.

Phebe is playing with the skipping rope. Nurinder asks to play and Phebe says "No!"

How does each child feel? (Discuss each scenario separately.)

In Someone Else's Shoes

How would you feel if this happened to you?

....
....
....

How would you feel if you had to go here?

....
....
....

How does this person feel?

....
....
....

'In Someone Else's Shoes' means

....
....

Name: .... Date: ....

Activity

Social Skills Learning

Paying Compliments

Session aim
To identify the importance of paying compliments

Objectives
1. To identify three compliments
2. To discuss why compliments are important
3. To demonstrate appropriate ways to pay a compliment

Resources
- Ball
- Emotions cards (see Suggested Resources page 82)
- Scenarios (see page 53)

Session Plan

0 – 10 minutes	Ask the pupils how their day has been and if they would like to share one positive thing about it so far.
11 – 30 minutes	Give each pupil a compliment about their behaviour and listening skills. Explain that whoever gets the ball will say a compliment about who they are passing it to. Then ask the pupils to use the emotions cards to identify how they felt when they received a compliment.
31 – 50 minutes	Read out the scenarios and ask the pupils to role-play these different social situations which may require compliments.
51 – 60 minutes	Pupils complete the Paying Compliments worksheet.

Social Skills Learning

Scenarios – Paying Compliments

Betty got 10/10 on her spellings.

It is Jack's birthday today.

Daniel has new shoes on today.

Social Skills Learning

Paying Compliments

A compliment is ....

....

Your friend is wearing a shirt you like.

What could you say?

Your teacher has had her hair cut.

What could you say?

Name: .... Date: ....

Just for Fun! 4

Are you up for the challenge ...?

What you need:

✓ Masking tape

✓ Straws

✓ Pompoms

✓ Scissors

1. Stick the tape to the table as a straight line, zigzag line and some other lines

2. Place the pompom at one end of the tape

3. Using your straw try to blow the pompom to the other side without it coming off the line

✓ How many times did you try before you succeeded? Think about the skills you used ...

Social Skills Learning

How do You Want to be Treated by Others?

Session aim
To identify how pupils would like to be treated by others

Objectives
1. To identify how pupils should treat others
2. To discuss why respect is important
3. To demonstrate respect

Resources
- Feelings cards (see Suggested Resources page 82)
- A3 paper
- Coloured pens

Session Plan

0 – 10 minutes	Ask the pupils how their day has been and to talk about one positive thing they have experienced.
11 – 20 minutes	Role-play an argument with a member of staff, demonstrating this person not sharing and being unhelpful. Ask the pupils to explain how it made them feel seeing the staff argue and mistreat each other. Use feelings cards for support. Ask the pupils how the situation could have been handled differently.
21 – 40 minutes	Use A3 paper to make a thought shower. Give the pupils the opportunity to reflect on times when they were not treated fairly by others. Ask them to reflect on how they treat others and if they feel they need to change the way they treat others.
41 – 60/65 minutes	Pupils complete the How do You Want to be Treated by Others? worksheet.

How do You Want to be Treated by Others?

If someone does the following to you what could you do?

1. Calls you a name

....

2. Shouts at you

....

3. Says they do not want to hang around with you

....

4. Will not share

....

How do you want to be treated by others?

....

How should you treat others?

....

Name: .... Date: ....

Social Skills Learning

Listening

Session aim	
To promote active listening skills	
Objectives	
1. To identify active listening skills	
2. To discuss why listening is important	
3. To demonstrate effective listening skills	

Resources
- Blindfold
- Pictures of body parts e.g. eyes, ears, face (see page 59)

Session Plan

0 – 10 minutes	Ask the pupils how their day has been and to identify one good thing about it.
11 – 20 minutes	Choose a pupil to be guided around the room blindfolded; choose another to instruct them safely from one side of the room to the other. **Please carry out a risk assessment of the environment before beginning this activity. Also exercise caution regarding children who may not wish to be blindfolded. Staff should demonstrate this first.** **Explain health and safety and check that the pupils know their right and left sides.**
21 – 40 minutes	Ask the pupils to identify how they can show they are listening by using the different body parts as a point of reference e.g. eyes = eye contact.
41 – 50 minutes	Ask the pupils to show positive body language and active listening skills one at a time. Praise them for showing they are listening to instructions throughout the session.
51 – 60 minutes	Pupils complete the Listening worksheet.

Activity

Listening

Social Skills Learning

Listening

What is a good listener?

....

What is a bad listener?

....

Are you a good or bad listener? ....

Circle True or False ...

1. A good listener rushes the person speaking

True or False?

2. A good listener looks at the person speaking to them

True or False?

3. A good listener interrupts a person

True or False?

4. A bad listener asks appropriate questions

True or False?

Name: .... Date: ....

Healthy Eating

Session aim
To discuss the importance of a balanced diet

Objectives
1. To be able to identify what a healthy meal consists of
2. To consider the importance of regular meals throughout the day

Resources
- Interactive whiteboard
- Whiteboards and marker pens
- Eatwell plate – see page 62 but check www.nhs.uk/Livewell/Goodfood/Pages/eatwell-plate.aspx for the latest version
- Paper plates
- Plastic food/cardboard food boxes

Session Plan

0 – 15 minutes	Ask the pupils how their day has been and if they would like to share one good thing about it.
16 – 25 minutes	Recognise, identify, label and define the five food groups using the Eatwell plate (this can be done on an interactive whiteboard). Identify which groups foods belong to. Extension task: list, on any whiteboard, as many foods as possible in each food group, when asked.
26 – 30 minutes	Using the Eatwell plate, create a healthy meal. This could be drawn or written on the paper plates or by arranging the empty containers appropriately. The pupils can work individually or in groups as appropriate.
31 – 45 minutes	Create two other healthy meals of the day.
46 – 60 minutes	Pupils complete the Healthy Eating worksheet.

Social Skills Learning

The eatwell plate

Healthy Eating

How many meals should you eat per day?
....

How many calories should you have per day?
....

Draw a healthy meal below:

```
┌─────────────────────────────────────┐
│                                     │
│                                     │
│                                     │
│                                     │
└─────────────────────────────────────┘
```

Are you a healthy eater?   YES/NO

Why? ....

Write one new healthy eating goal below:

1. ....

Name: ....   Date: ....

Social Skills Learning

Personal Hygiene

Session aim

To gain knowledge of basic hygiene practices

Objectives

1. To identify what facilities are used to uphold personal hygiene
2. To discuss why personal hygiene is important
3. To demonstrate good practice regarding washing hands effectively

Resources

- Personal hygiene true/false statements and cards from page 65
- Looking After Your Body fact sheet on page 66
- YouTube clip http://www.youtube.com/watch?v=bAwS0UslEDs
- Interactive whiteboard
- Liquid handwash
- Water and bowl
- Paper towels

Session Plan

0 – 10 minutes	Ask the pupils how their day has been and if they would like to share one positive thing about it.
11 – 20 minutes	Start the lesson by stating key facts/fiction about personal hygiene using the statements on page 65 and ask the pupils to decide whether they are true/false using their cards.
21 – 30 minutes	Ask the pupils to give examples of how to look after their body properly. Ask them what illnesses they could get from not looking after their body properly (refer to the Looking After Your Body fact sheet and hand it out if you wish).
31 – 45 minutes	Ask the pupils to watch the YouTube clip demonstrating how to wash their hands correctly. You could put it up on an interactive whiteboard. Then everyone should give it a try.
46 – 60 minutes	Pupils complete the Personal Hygiene worksheet.

Personal Hygiene – True/False?

1. Looking after your body is very important.
True or False?

2. If you do not look after your body it is ok, you will not get ill/poorly.
True or False?

3. Not having a wash for three days does not mean you will smell.
True or False?

4. Regularly washing your hair and cutting your nails is important.
True or False?

5. Brushing your teeth twice a day will stop tooth loss/decay/bad breath.
True or False?

Looking After Your Body

- Touching the hands, clothing or bodies of people with poor hygiene spreads colds, ringworm, head and body lice, and other parasites and viruses

- Not brushing your teeth can result in having bad breath and tooth loss/decay

- Making sure you wear deodorant will minimise the effects of bad body odour

- Washing your body with soap/shower gel on a daily basis and drying away the water properly so it is not hot and damp between your toes will reduce the risk of spreading nail infections

Social Skills Learning

Worksheet

Personal Hygiene

Link each part of the body to the actions which keep them clean.

Hand 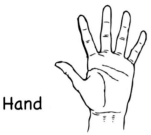　　　 Bath

Nose 　　　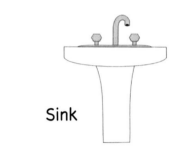 Sink

Teeth 　　　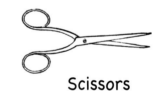 Scissors

Body 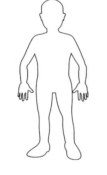　　　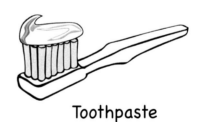 Toothpaste

Nails 　　　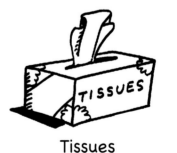 Tissues

Name: ....　Date: ....

Just for Fun! 5

All bottled up ...

What you need:

✓ Different coloured sand

✓ Small bottles

✓ Masking tape

✓ Scissors

✓ Newspaper

1. Cover the table with newspaper
2. Put different coloured layers of sand into a bottle
3. Tape the lid on securely

✓ What could the colours represent about what you keep bottled up ...?

....

....

....

....

Activity

Growing Pains

Session aim
To identify emotional changes in different stages of life
Objectives
1. To discuss emotional changes experienced linked to growing up
2. To identify strategies for coping with emotional changes

Resources
• Emotional changes flashcards (see http://www.twinkl.co.uk/resource/t-t-189-ourselves-emotion-flashcards-parents)
• Relaxation cards (see Suggested Resources page 82)

Session Plan

0 – 10 minutes	Ask the pupils one by one how their day has been and if they can share one good thing about it.
11 – 25 minutes	Split the group into pairs and give each one of the pair three of the descriptions from the list on the following page. Ask them to stick each description on the emotions face which may show the particular emotional changes: - Sadness - Loss of interest in hobbies - Tiredness - Irritability - Anxiety - School performance decline
26 – 40 minutes	Demonstrate the following breathing relaxation technique which may help if pupils feel anxious (make sure they are sitting down): 1) Place one hand on your chest 2) Place the other hand on your stomach 3) Breathe in through your nose 4) Breathe out through your mouth 5) Repeat six times Discuss other ways they could relax using the relaxation cards e.g.: - Going for a walk - Doing exercise - Playing sport - Socialising with friends and family
41 – 60 minutes	Pupils complete the Growing Pains worksheet.

Emotions

Sadness

Loss of interest in hobbies

Tiredness

Irritability

Anxiety

School performance decline

Growing Pains

Tick your social and emotional changes so far.

Boys and girls

☐ mood swings may happen when strong feelings change from happy to sad to angry in a way that might be hard to understand

☐ feelings about self (self-esteem) may change

☐ may take more risks

☐ think about body changes a lot

☐ want to do things without help and try to be independent

☐ want to have privacy and be alone

☐ have strong sexual feelings

☐ may want to have or be with friends more

Name: .... Date: ....

Activity

Appropriate Language

Session aim
To identify appropriate language
Objective
To identify three types of language which can be used in specific contexts/settings

Resources
• Small tubes of toothpaste • Picture cards of positive role models e.g. police, teachers, family members and negative role models such as a robber, someone pushing another person • Cards of appropriate language e.g. thank you, please, OK, excuse me, I'm sorry (see page 73) • Social story (you can find these on the Internet and see Suggested Resources) • Finger puppets

Session Plan

0 – 10 minutes	Ask all the pupils to say one positive thing about their day and give them the opportunity to explain why if they would like to do so.
11 – 20 minutes	Show them the toothpaste and demonstrate squeezing all of the toothpaste out of the tube. Give the pupils the opportunity to do this also; once completed give them the challenge of getting it back in. Link this to words and not being able to take back words which may be hurtful.
21 – 30 minutes	Ask the pupils to split the picture cards into two groups, one of positive and the other of negative role models.
31 – 50 minutes	Give the pupils the word cards and ask them to lift up the appropriate card as you re-enact a social story using the finger puppets.
51 – 60 minutes	Pupils complete the Appropriate Language worksheet with support if necessary.

Appropriate Language Cards

please

thank you

OK

excuse me

I'm sorry

Social Skills Learning

Appropriate Language

What type of words should you not say in school?

....

....

....

Have you said words which you should not have said before?

....

....

....

How may it make your friends or a member of staff feel if you use inappropriate words?

....

....

....

What words can you say instead?

....

....

....

Name: .... Date: ....

Social Skills Learning

What I Have Learned

Session aim
To reflect on learning

Objectives
1. To identify one thing which the pupils have enjoyed
2. To discuss one thing which they have found hard to understand

Resources
- Pens
- Coloured pens/pencil

Session Plan

0 – 10 minutes	Ask all the pupils to say one positive thing about their day and give them the opportunity to explain why if they would like to do so.
11 – 30 minutes	Let them look through their tasks and worksheets to see all the work they have completed to give them the opportunity to reflect on their learning.
31 – 50 minutes	Give the pupils the opportunity to express what they have learned (through writing or drawing) and enjoyed throughout the sessions as well as what they would like to understand more about.
51 – 60 minutes	Pupils complete the What I Have Learned worksheet with support if necessary.

Social Skills Learning

What I Have Learned...

Name: .... Date: ....

Just for Fun! 6

My journey ...

What you need:

- ✓ Newspaper
- ✓ Masking tape
- ✓ Paint
- ✓ PVA glue
- ✓ Pen
- ✓ Paintbrush
- ✓ Masks, see page 3 or search the Internet for free downloads

1. Cover the table with newspaper
2. Choose your mask
3. Rip the newspaper into strips
4. Paint the newspaper strips onto the mask in crumples and layers
5. Leave to dry
6. Paint shapes and use colours to symbolise your social skills journey so far

- ✓ Think about what you have learned and how you can use your learning in the future ...

Appendices

Social Skills Learning

My Social Skills Workbook

Stick a picture of yourself here

This book belongs to

....

Class

....

Pupil Tracking Sheet
Social Skills Learning

Name: ....

Session: ....

Please evidence assessed criteria using examples such as an account of group discussion, peer assessment, photographs, observations, multiple-choice assessment and role-play

Not Met:

Assessor Name: Date:

Partially Met:

Assessor Name: Date:

Fully Achieved:

Assessor Name: Date:

Suggested Resources

Emotions Faces/Changes Cards

Emotions Cards (www.loggerheadpublishing.co.uk)

Emotions ColorCards (www.speechmark.net)

Emotions & Expressions ColorCards (www.speechmark.net)

Feelings Cards

Feelings Cards (www.loggerheadpublishing.co.uk)

Feelings ColorCards (www.speechmark.net)

Following and Breaking Rules

Hidden Rules (www.childswork.com)

Expressions Cards

Emotions & Expressions ColorCards (www.speechmark.net)

Relaxation Cards

Relaxation Cards (www.relaxkids.com)

Social Stories

Gray, Carol (2001) *My Social Stories Book*, Jessica Kingsley Publishers.

Gray, Carol (2010) *The New Social Story Book*, Future Horizons.

Notes

Social Skills Learning

Other useful resources from Loggerhead Publishing

Emotions Cards

These carefully selected cards focus on emotions - both positive and negative - and can be used in many different ways.

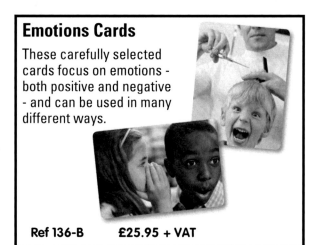

Ref 136-B   £25.95 + VAT

Dingle Duck

By Liz Morris

Cards to help children develop sound self-esteem and excellent social and emotional skills.

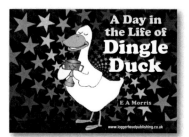

Ref 165-B   £27.50 + VAT

This is My Book Series

Worksheet-based activity books that will help children understand themselves better, consider the world around them in more depth, improve their relationships, try to solve problems and think about how to realise their dreams.

Ref 164-B   £94.75

Feelings Cards

Develop important social, emotional and behavioural skills with this resource.

Ref 033-B   £24.95 + VAT

Understanding Your Emotions CD-Rom

By Sue Neame & Ashley Ross

Promote emotional well-being in children through these interesting activities backed up by lesson plans and information.

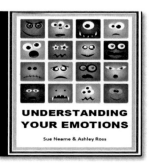

Ref 2-140-B   £39.95 + VAT

To place an order or for more details please call +44 (0)1604 870828, email: orders@loggerheadpublishing.co.uk or visit www.loggerheadpublishing.co.uk